Negotiation: Modern business wouldn't exist without it. We negotiate all the time without realizing it. We negotiate our salaries when we take a job. We negotiate our hours every day, even if it's only to get an extra hour at lunch to take our kid to ball practice.

Some people are gifted negotiators. Some aren't.

Yet everyone can learn the basics of negotiation—and everyone can become good at it, maybe even brilliant. And the key is not, as some will tell you, to be fearless. The key is to know what you want.

How to Negotiate Anything

A Freelancer's Survival Guide Short Book

Kristine Kathryn Rusch

wMG
Publishing

List of all the
Freelancer's Survival Guide
Short Books

When to Quit Your Day Job
Getting Started
Turning Setbacks into Opportunity
Goals and Dreams
How to Negotiate Anything
The Secrets of Success
How to Make Money
Networking in Person and Online
Time Management

How to Negotiate Anything
A Freelancer's Survival Guide Short Book

Copyright © 2012 Kristine Kathryn Rusch

All rights reserved

Published 2012 by WMG Publishing
www.wmgpublishing.com
Cover art © copyright Leo Blanchette/Dreamstime
Book and cover design copyright © 2012 WMG Publishing

WMG Publishing
www.wmgpublishing.com

Table of Contents

How to Negotiate Anything

A Freelancer's Survival Guide Short Book

Kristine Kathryn Rusch

Introduction

Negotiation: Modern business wouldn't exist without it. We negotiate all the time without realizing it. We negotiate our salaries when we take a job. We negotiate our hours every day, even if it's only to get an extra hour at lunch to take our kid to ball practice.

Some people are gifted negotiators. Some aren't.

Yet everyone can learn the basics of negotiation—and everyone can become good at it, maybe even brilliant. And the key is not, as some will tell you, to be fearless. The key is to know what you want.

This *Freelancer's Survival Guide* short book will teach you everything you need to know about negotiation. It will help you in small situations—like that hour off—and in big ones such as negotiating a contract.

The sections of this short book were originally written for *The Freelancer's Survival Guide*, which originated on my blog, kristinekathrynrusch.com. The *Guide* has morphed into a series of short books. The full *Guide* will be published in the fall of 2010 in both electronic and paperback editions.

The short books exist for people who don't want all 130,000 words of the *Guide*. Those people don't need help with all aspects of their freelance business, only with a few aspects. If all you need is to learn how to negotiate, then this short book is for you.

The segments in this short book were written on a weekly basis, and I've tried to maintain that conversational flavor. Enjoy the book. I hope it helps you in all of your important negotiations.

— Kristine Kathryn Rusch
Lincoln City, Oregon
August 28, 2010

The Rules of Negotiation

My ex-husband used to say all of life is negotiable. That attitude fascinated me and repelled me at the same time. I loved the way he could get bargains, and I loved the way he refused to hear the word no. But I was raised by people who didn't negotiate. For all I know, my parents spent full list price on their cars.

The price was the price, my upbringing said. When someone told you the rules, you followed them. You didn't negotiate them. You didn't ask for the price to come down. You didn't try to get something special for yourself.

Who did you think you were, anyway? Someone *special*? Someone to whom the rules did not apply?

My husband, Dean Wesley Smith, also loves to negotiate. He hates to spend full price for anything. Early in our relationship, I argued with him as he tried to negotiate the price of a television set in a Fred Meyer store. Fred Meyer, for those of you who don't live near one, was once considered a lower-level department store. Now it's mid-level. It sells everything from food to electronics to clothes to furniture, but not as cheaply as Wal-Mart or Target nor as expensively as Macy's. What Fred Meyer shares with those places is this: the listed price is the price. If they want to discount the item, they put it on sale.

Dean never believed that. He knew that the salesperson on the floor couldn't negotiate, but the manager could. So Dean would see the last television set or the single remaining display model or a huge number of televisions, none of which were moving, and he'd ask for the manager. Then Dean would offer to pay half price and take the item away immediately— no box, no nothing. Just cash.

Nine times out of ten, the manager took him up on the offer. Or she'd negotiate in return. *I can't sell you that television at half price, but I can sell you this one for even less.*

Some places—like car dealerships—expect you to negotiate. When I lived in Madison, Wisconsin, there was an appliance and electronics store called American Furniture and Appliances, run by a guy named Lenny. Everyone in town called the place Crazy TV Lenny's because that was the moniker that he gave himself on his wild TV ads (for an idea what this guy was like, see the Ted Danson character in *Made in America*).

My ex and I often shopped there, and I let my ex handle the negotiations. His mother gave us $200 every Christmas, and we managed to stretch it a long way—often through my ex's negotiating skill at Crazy TV Lenny's.

Even there, I had trouble listening to the negotiation. But I knew it was appropriate.

It wasn't appropriate (or so I believed) at Fred Meyer. So, on that night more than twenty years ago, as Dean started into his negotiations, I hissed at him: "They don't negotiate here."

He waved me off.

"Seriously," I said. "They won't let you do that here."

Finally, he turned to me and snapped, "Kindly shut up."

Which I did, surprisingly enough.

And we walked out with a much-needed $500 television that we only paid $200 for.

You can negotiate anywhere. The worst thing they can say to you is no.

Back then, my problem with face-to-face negotiation was a case of terminal embarrassment. I didn't want to call attention to myself in public in anyway. Some of this came from my shyness, but some of it came from my upbringing. My mother worried constantly about what other people thought, and it rubbed off on me. It still takes a conscious effort for me not to worry about what other people think.

I figured if it was bad form to negotiate, then people would remember, and ostracize me.

Only no one has ever remembered Dean badly for negotiation. In fact, the places he's negotiated things have remembered him, and have often offered him other deals. They *respect* him, which was quite a lesson for me.

The other lesson about face-to-face negotiation that I learned from both men is that both of them negotiated with a smile and a shrug. They charmed the salesperson, making the salesperson feel as good about the sale as they did.

Now, no one has ever called me charming. Strong, opinionated, blunt, difficult, smart, and truthful, yes, but charming—never. And honestly, while I care what people think as a default mode, I mostly don't care if they like me. I am what I am: take it or leave it.

The charmer makes each person feel special. And the charmer can be a chameleon, becoming all things to all people.

Sadly, I don't have the patience for that. A charmer can negotiate face-to-face from a position of weakness.

I can't—at least not face-to-face. I can negotiate from a position of weakness in writing or through an intermediary. More on that later.

I can, however, negotiate face-to-face if I believe it's a matter of fairness. Which was why I had no trouble as a sixteen-year-old asking for payment for my high school newspaper column. It seemed logical to me that if everyone else at the paper got paid for their work, I should as well. I presented it that way to my teacher, who presented to the paper. I didn't try to charm anyone.

I've done that many times over the years. I do it from an informed perspective. I find out what others get paid for the same work and ask for that rate for myself. Or ask for an increase based on past performance.

I have no trouble doing that. It's based on rules, you see, and I can do rules face-to-face.

But things like negotiating at a car dealership or in a store have no rules, so I'm at a loss. I don't do it, but these days, I'm happy when Dean does—and occasionally I suggest it to him. Then I leave the vicinity. Because I can't stay calm while he does it. I panic or get embarrassed, even now.

Which is why I initially put off writing about negotiation. I don't do it well face-to-face. I think of Dean or my ex-husband. I think of all those other people I've known who are experts at getting the best price for the best product, and I know I'm not like them.

However, if you were to ask anyone who does business with me, they'd call me a skilled negotiator. In fact, I've had a number of people tell me I'm such a good negotiator, I should do it for a living—as a book agent, for example. (Which means they aren't thinking things through. Why should I make 15% off someone else's work, when I can make 85 to 100% off my own?)

How can I be known as such a skilled negotiator when I can't dicker with a car dealer?

Simple: I know my strengths and weaknesses. I also know what I want.

The rules for negotiation are pretty easy:

1. Know What You Want

That sounds elementary, but most people don't know what they want before they enter into negotiation. In the TV example above, Dean and I were broke, with only about $250 to our name. Our television had died a spectacular death (involving sparks and explosions), and we needed a new one. We wanted the best set we could get for our money. Me, I would have just looked at $200 TVs. Dean looked at all the TVs to see which he could bargain down to $200. He got us the better deal. But we knew our limits. We couldn't spend more than $200 and still get groceries. I'm sure the store manager had some kind of limitation on his end as well—probably the cost of the item versus the cost of the space it took on his shelf.

2. Ask.

You won't get what you want if you don't ask, so what's the risk? The worst thing the other party can do is say no.

3. Be Prepared To Walk Away.

You won't always get what you want. But you should never settle for less than what you need. So many people get caught up in the negotiation they forget that they can simply say no and leave. You can always try another day.

4. Stay Calm.

Negotiations are for rational people, making business decisions. The moment you feel yourself getting angry or panicked or embarrassed, end the negotiation. Calm down. You have to be able to think clearly, and you won't be able to do that if you're emotional in any way.

5. Never Reveal Your Entire Hand.

Even if you're desperate—especially if you're desperate—don't admit it. Don't tell the salesperson that you only have $200. Don't say you'll do anything to be published or start your business or go on TV. The moment you reveal your deepest needs, you give the other party a hook that will guarantee that they'll triumph in the negotiation. Make sure that you keep your reasons for making the deal—whatever it is—completely to yourself.

6. Don't Flip-Flop.

If you say you'll walk before you spend $250, then walk. Make promises and keep them. Or you lose your standing in the negotiation, and your word means nothing.

All of this is deliberately vague, because negotiation happens in a variety of circumstances. You negotiate salary when you get a job, as does your future boss. You negotiate when you propose marriage to someone—you are making an alliance, after all, and you discuss what that alliance entails. You negotiate when you rent an apartment or buy a house. You negotiate when you order in large quantities from a supplier. Most of us even negotiate traffic tickets ("Honest, officer, I didn't see the speed limit sign. It's hidden behind a bush.")

Each of those negotiations takes different skills.

So for the sake of the *Guide*, I'll examine the most common types of negotiation you'll do when you're in business. These include—but are not limited to—contracts and financial dealings. I'll also discuss negotiations with potential clients and with potential employees.

All of these take different approaches. For example, fiduciary negotiations might be short-term, like my high school column for the local paper. But contracts exist for the length of that contract—anywhere from six months to ten years or more. You need to think about all aspects of that as you negotiate, not just your short-term goal.

Then there are different methods of negotiation. Many of us hire a negotiator—be that an agent or an attorney or a publicist—to do the actual talking for us. But a negotiator needs guidance, and ultimately, they're following *your* wishes. So I'll discuss when you need one and when you don't. And when you do need one, what kind should you hire? A charmer, a shark, or a combination of both?

Negotiation is a deep topic. The first thing you need to do as we delve into it is figure out how good you are at negotiating. Can you negotiate face-to-face? Is it easy for you to ask for what you want? When you do ask, do you get it nine out of ten times or do you alienate the people you talk to?

Before you enter a negotiation, you also need to figure out something else: The power relationships.

In each relationship, one person has more power than the other person. Most recently, I heard this premise expressed in a fairly mediocre Matthew McConaughey movie called *The Ghosts of Girlfriends Past*. Michael Douglas, in the Jacob Marley role (and frankly, the best thing in the movie), tells McConaughey that the person with the most power in any romantic relationship is the person who wants it the *least*.

If you think about that, that's true. The person who is the least involved controls whether or not the relationship continues. The other person, the person who wants it the most, must abide by the wishes of the person who doesn't want it quite as much.

But as McConaughey learns in the movie, romantic relations aren't (or shouldn't be) about power. They're about a lot of other things, not the least of which are love and friendship and valuing the other person.

I didn't tell you this just for your sappy movie lesson of the day, but for that one little nugget of truth spoken by Douglas's character. In any negotiation, the person who wants it the least has the most power.

Job seekers are discovering this right now. They really, really, really need a job, any job (the higher paying the better), so that the bills get paid. Employers, on the other hand, aren't sure about the wisdom of hiring yet another employee, so employers approach the negotiation with ambivalence.

When ambivalence meets desperation, one of two things occurs. Either the ambivalent person decides it's too much work to hire someone—particularly when a lot of job seekers answer an ad—or the ambivalent one takes advantage of another person's desperation. Desperate people say things like,

"I'll do anything," or "Just hire me, please." And that leads to being underpaid for the job or overworked, just to please the boss—if, of course, the boss chooses to hire.

The set-up question for this often comes early in the interview, by the way. It's the "what kind of salary would you like?" question, which was a question I always hated as a job seeker and refused to answer. What I would say was either, "You stated your pay rates in the ad, which is why I answered it" or "Perhaps you should tell me what you're willing to pay." The first answer shut down that fishing question; the second threw the ball back into the interviewer's court.

When I mentioned that question at a weekly writers' lunch the other day (in connection with writing about negotiation), a woman who has worked at middle-management jobs her whole life said her answer to the question was similar to mine: "What are you willing to pay?"

But the best answer came from a man who worked in the highest level of management for decades, getting six-figure salaries in the computer industry. He said whenever he got asked that question, he would respond, "We can discuss that later. Let's see first if we're suited for each other."

Invariably at the end of the interview, when the company indicated that they wanted to hire him—and he wanted to work for them—the company would ask again what kind of salary he wanted. He would respond, "I'd like to get more than I'm being paid now."

Of course, they'd ask his current rate, and choke when they heard it. But, he said, they always paid him. By the end of his high-tech career, he often got paid more than his bosses.

That's a skilled negotiator.

Note in his example the fluidity of the power relationship. In the beginning, the power seemed to belong to the hiring company. Then they asked the salary question. He made it clear that he wasn't even sure he wanted the job. The power relationship became equal at that point. The discussions continued, and eventually, the company decided that they wanted him. He then had the power in the relationship—he could say no. And he stated his terms, which were "Pay me more than I'm getting now."

In other words, he didn't need them, but they needed him.

So many people can't do that because they need the job itself. So you have to understand when you enter into that negotiation that you (the potential employee) automatically have less power in the negotiation. You *need* the job. They *want* an employee, but they don't necessarily want you.

You need to convince them to hire you without being desperate about it. And you probably won't be in position to argue over salary. Which was always my position when I was looking for a day job. I never wanted a day job, so I only applied when I needed one. Look again at my answers to that question. "What's your salary range?" Or "I saw your range in the ad, and that's why I'm here."

In other words, I took salary off the table, let them know they could afford me, and then we figured out if they wanted to hire me (and if I wanted to be hired. Even desperate, I knew there were jobs I couldn't [or shouldn't] do).

I've watched this same dynamic play out with writers over the years. Freelance fiction writers, who have struggled for years, often accept the first offer they receive on a book. In publishing, the first offer a new writer gets is a low-ball offer. The editor expects the writer to negotiate. In fact, the editor who makes the offer *wants* the writer to negotiate because, if writer doesn't, the editor knows the writer will hate the publisher later. The writer will end up blaming the publishing company for "screwing" him when really, the writer screwed himself by not negotiating.

But in that early publishing relationship, the publishing company does have more power. They have it in two ways: they have the resources to publish the book; and they've become the vehicle for fulfilling a writer's greatest dream. It takes guts and a firm belief in one's self to walk away from that, but the writers who do benefit later on.

In the writer/publisher relationship, the power shifts over time. An established writer will often not get book offers because the editor is afraid to anger the writer with a low-ball offer. (I always say, *Make the offer, and let me make the decision.*) Established writers have a lot more clout than new writers.

I think that the only time that writers and publishers reach parity is in the case of established writers who are negotiating with their publishers. They're negotiating over the book itself, and the power lines are equal. The writer wants the sale, yes, but only under certain conditions. The publisher wants the book, yes, but only under certain conditions. And the writer and publisher must then negotiate the best deal for all involved.

Bestselling writers and writers with hot properties, however, have all of the power in the publishing industry (many of them just don't realize it). They command higher advances, promotion budgets, and so on. They get offers from other publishing houses trying to steal them away. These authors sometimes won't get offers from the houses that want them because those houses really and truly can't afford them. And everyone, everyone, wants a piece of those authors, so the authors can set their price.

Power fluctuates. You just have to know what yours is when you enter into a negotiation. Now let's look at negotiations themselves.

Negotiating for the Short Term

In the last section, I mentioned how Dean negotiated for a television set. That was a short-term negotiation. We needed a TV, we had limited dollars, and we wanted that TV immediately. So, we went with a set price in mind. Dean got us the best TV he could find for our limited dollars.

End of negotiation, end of situation.

You encounter this all the time as a freelancer. Someone wants to hire you for a short-term project. Or you want to work on a short-term project. This is a one-time thing that has absolutely no resale value. That's important because in many kinds of freelancing, your work can be sold and resold for years to come. Artists, writers, and musicians, in particular, face the resale issue, but not in every case.

So, let's put this in a musician's ballpark. A few blocks from my house is one of the best blues clubs in the Northwest. Up-and-coming groups play there as well as long-term professionals and extremely famous blues musicians.

The gigs are short—one or two nights—and since no one is allowed to record while the musicians are playing, the gigs have no resale value at all. It's just a group of musicians playing to a crowded club.

Sometimes when musicians play bars, there are contracts. Sometimes there aren't. In this hypothetical case, let's assume there are no contracts involved. Just a handshake.

Musicians can get a flat fee for playing. They can get a flat fee and a percentage of the cover charge (if there is one). (A cover charge, for those of you who don't know, is the price you pay just to get into the club. Some clubs charge these every night; some never charge it; and some charge it only when there's a big name group playing.) Musicians can get a flat fee and a percentage of the bar's earnings that night. They can get a flat fee, a percentage of cover, *and* a percentage of the bar's earnings. Or they can get a percentage of cover and the bar's earnings. Or just a percentage of cover…

You see how this goes. It's all negotiable.

A brand new torch singer with no following at all might ask for a percentage of cover and the bar's earnings, but that's probably not wise for the bar or the singer. Because a brand new singer has no following, charging cover is probably a mistake—unless the club is so exclusive that playing there is an honor that will launch the torch singer's career. Even then, the torch singer should probably negotiate a flat fee. After all, this is a limited engagement and attendance will probably be down. The torch singer has a better chance of making her expenses with the flat fee than with a percentage.

However, the established professional probably wants a combination—a small guarantee (in other words, a flat fee) plus percentages of the cover and the bar's take. The small guarantee pays for everything should it be a stormy night or the advertising failed and the club didn't fill up.

The Big Names have an appearance fee that is non-negotiable (except for real friends). That gets paid no matter what. Whether it comes out of the cover or the bar's earnings, it doesn't matter. The appearance fee gets paid. However, some Big Names want the appearance fee and a percentage of cover and the bar's earnings.

If you look at this, you realize that when a club books a Big Name, the club could actually lose money on the appearance. Why would a club do that? To bring in new customers, and hope they become repeat customers.

(This happens in books as well, which is why bestselling books are often sold at a discount. That's to bring people into the bookstore with the hope that they'll buy other books.)

But let's go back to our brand-new torch singer. She can ask for the same appearance fee as the Big Name, but she won't get it. In fact, she might get laughed at. She can take the flat fee the club offers. She can take a percentage of cover and bar, with the idea that she might not make any money.

Most beginners wouldn't ask for the Big Name's appearance fee, not because they're afraid of being laughed at, but because they wouldn't think of it. Fine. That's probably good.

Okay. So, we know what the power relationship is in this instance. But now let's look at the other part of the negotiation.

1. *What Does Our Torch Singer Want?*

She needs to figure out what she wants more than anything else. Is this club prestigious? Will it launch her career? Or is it just a local club in a small town that really has no importance at all?

If it's an important club and she wants to play the club more than anything else—money, hours, anything—then she has to make sure to keep that firmly in mind before she negotiates anything.

But let's assume this is a local club. Now she has to figure out what she wants to get paid. Let's also assume that the gig is two nights—Friday and Saturday—with no hope of renewal. She needs to find out how much the cover is, if there even is a cover, and what the bar expects to earn. Sometimes she can do that in her head—the number of seats in the club times the cover price plus the cost of one drink. If that number turns out to be much higher in a full club than the flat fee, she might want to ask for that. Of course, the request assumes she'll fill the club, which she probably won't, considering that it's a local club and she's an unknown.

But she is taking a risk with the club owner, and they both have a stake in a good outcome. It might be worth the gamble to her.

Let's assume, though, that her rent is past due. She needs money more than anything else. She needs the flat fee at the very minimum.

Our torch singer has decided she needs a flat fee to play at the local club on Friday and Saturday night. That's the bottom line of her negotiation.

2. *Ask.*

But she needs money, and the flat fee is a small amount— say $100 for two nights. She gets the practice, and she's not going to say no to the $100. Does she tell the club owner that at the beginning of the negotiation? Of course not.

She has done her research, though, and she has learned that this club doesn't charge a cover when the performer is unknown.

So, she goes into the negotiation knowing her limits: she can't ask for a cover percentage and she needs the flat fee. But it would be nice if she made more money than that flat fee.

She asks for a $200 flat fee. That's double what was offered, but it's worth a try. But it would be better for her to ask for the flat fee plus a percentage of the bar. Because if she's good and word gets around, Saturday's bar take should be pretty high. She's taking a risk along with the club owner. She's not costing him extra money if no one comes to her performances, and she's making money if people do.

So she asks. What's the worst thing the club owner can say? All together now…the worst thing he can say is no.

3. *Be Prepared to Walk Away.*

In this particular instance, our torch singer is *not* prepared to walk away. She needs the money. But she doesn't tell the club owner that. The nuclear option is not available to her.

He's probably willing to walk away. So if he says no to her request for a percentage of the bar, she should laugh, tell him that $100 is fine, and shake hands.

4. *Stay Calm.*

She needs that $100. Is she nervous? You bet. Can she negotiate? I hope so. But she's a performer. She can probably pretend calm when she doesn't have it. If she can't pretend, then she should take a few deep breaths and make sure she thinks about each sentence before she speaks.

Because at her level of the career, it would be foolish for her to hire a manager to do the negotiating for her. Better that she learn how to do it on her own than sacrifice $15 to $20 of that much needed $100 for someone to speak for her—when she wouldn't get much out of that deal anyway.

5. *Never Reveal Your Entire Hand.*

Let's assume the deal's done, the hands are shaken, the torch singer is going to play the club. Should she tell the club owner that she needed that $100 more than anything? No.

Should she tell him she never planned to walk away from the gig? No.

Because she might negotiate with him in the future, and she doesn't want him to know how good she is. She doesn't want to give him any insight into her ways of thinking. It doesn't benefit her—and he probably doesn't care anyway.

6. *Don't Flip-Flop.*

She's committed to the gig, shaken hands, and agreed to a fee. So she shouldn't arrive on Friday night, see that the club is full, and ask for more money. Nor should she back out of the deal, even if she finds out later that the club owner usually pays first-timers $500. She made the agreement; she should stick to it. If she doesn't like the deal, she needs to remember that *in future deals.* This one will be over in two days, she'll have some practice singing sexy songs in a dark club, and $100 toward her rent. That's what she negotiated, and if she's not satisfied, she needs to make sure she never agrees to this kind of deal again.

Which brings us back to point one. In future deals, she'll remember this deal and make sure she never takes a fee this low again—or does more research and finds out what others get paid—or agrees to only one night at $100.

This deal doesn't hurt her long-term. She has only short-term considerations: a two-night stint, a flat fee, a few songs.

Understanding Contracts

Negotiating for the long term is dicey. If you make a mistake, you don't have to live with it for a weekend. You might have to live with it for years.

So, before we discuss the specifics, let's talk about the emotions of negotiation.

On one of my e-mail lists, we're discussing taming your inner 12-year-old in a business situation. You know what I mean: the core you, the scared or angry or shy person hidden behind your adult façade.

Too many of us let our inner twelve-year-olds rule our life. My inner twelve-year-old is very shy. When I was twelve, I had switched schools from a pampered elitist school for the children of college professors to a public junior high school where the students occasionally carried knives. I was the victim of a horrible crime right after my twelfth birthday and was both traumatized and terrified throughout much of the year. For the first half of that school year, I came home from school and watched television until I went to bed; I didn't interact with anyone at all. People threatened me by their very existence. I survived by trying to predict their behavior.

And by being polite—very, very, very polite.

Extreme politeness is my default mode when I'm panicked. I'm very polite.

Fortunately, extreme politeness plus a need to predict behavior have made me a good negotiator. I plot out my moves and the other person's responses as if I'm plotting a Chose-Your-Own-Adventure novel. If other person does A, then I'll do A. If they do B, then I'll still do A. If they do C, I'll do B or K.

I rarely get surprised.

The problem for me in early negotiation—and in current negotiation if I'm not careful—isn't my inner twelve-year-old. It's my dreams. And dreams can catch anyone unaware.

If you're freelancing or thinking about freelancing, you love what you do. (If you don't love it, I have to ask you: why freelance?) In fact, you love what you do so much you've probably done it for free.

Money is rarely the freelancer's prime motivation. If it were, then people like Stephen Spielberg and Stephen King would retire after making their early millions. Even Donald

Trump, who claims he's interested in money, is only interested in money as a way of keeping score. He would have quit long ago if getting rich were his only motivation.

When you are doing something as a living and you would do that something for free, you have a conflict in the area of money. More often than not, you're willing to undervalue your product. And that's something you need to watch out for.

The flipside, however, is that when you get paid a lot of money for doing what you love, you'll continue doing that something. You won't be a rich, idle person, because you're not doing that something for the money. You're doing it for the love.

While this all may seem like a tangent to negotiation, it really isn't for several reasons. First, you need to know what your dreams for your business are and were, so that no one you're negotiating with can hook you in with those dreams. Second, you need to keep what you value the most about your work firmly in mind. And third, you have to know what your minimum nut is for your business.

If you haven't already done so, figure out what you need to keep your business running and to continue to make a living at it. If you don't know how to do that, order *How To Make Money: A Freelancer's Guide Short Book*. The book gives you tips in how to figure out exactly what you need for your business.

Once you have those numbers, you're still not ready to enter into the kinds of negotiation I'm going to talk about in this section. You'll also need to be completely aware of your inner twelve-year-old and her tendencies. (My inner twelve-year-old, when uncomfortable, either retreats entirely, gets very polite, or becomes unbelievably [and uncontrollably] rude.) You'll need to know your dreams. And you need to know what you want to accomplish in this particular negotiation.

I ran you through some of that in the last section about short-term negotiation. The negotiation described is relatively simple with very little on the line. The cost of making a mistake in that negotiation was no more than a weekend's worth of headache.

This section will deal with contractual negotiations.

Every freelancer will deal with contracts at some point or another. If you have a storefront, you'll make a contract for rent. If you provide product on a regular basis to other businesses, chances are you'll enter into a contract with them. If you hire independent contractors, you'll enter into a contract with them.

Most of us have gotten used to scanning the legalese we see online. We download something; we check "agree" at the bottom to expedite the process. But we've just agreed to something, and really, we should know what it is. Online, there generally is no negotiation. Either you agree or you don't get the service you want. But saying no is a viable option, one many of us don't take enough.

Contracts are negotiable. Sometimes you have a take-it-or-leave-it contract, like those agreements online, but that still means you have a choice. You don't have to sign.

In the past year, as I've read more and more articles about the foreclosure crisis, I've been struck by some similarities in the stories of borrowers who ended up underwater in their mortgages or who couldn't make their payments. Many of them thought that they *had* to sign the contract for the house purchase when they were presented with it. Several of them, particularly people dealing with some companies that specialized in fraud, didn't even know the terms of the contract until they'd signed it.

Most of these people in these articles were blue-collar workers, many of them without a high school education. But a large number were college graduates who had somehow never gotten the message that you shouldn't sign something you don't understand.

I'm assuming you guys know that.

But how many of you, when faced with pages and pages of contractual agreements, signed anyway? The day Dean and I completed a refinance on our house, we annoyed the people at the title company something awful. We refinanced in the middle of the housing boom, taking advantage of loose credit because as freelancers we hadn't been able to receive a bank-funded mortgage in periods of tight credit. (The previous owner carried our contract initially.)

Dean and I both insisted on reading the documents before us. We're good at scanning contracts—Dean went to law school, and I've been reading these puppies for years—and we went through them relatively quickly. Still, the woman with the title company kept looking at her watch and hurrying us along, telling us that some of the documents weren't very important.

We refused to sign one document because it changed the terms of our loan, the terms we had agreed to when we made the deal. In fact, it changed our loan from a fixed-rate mortgage to an adjustable-rate mortgage.

We made her draw up the paperwork all over again.

That document was slipped into the middle of about 100 pages of material.

I wonder how many other people that happened to, people who hadn't read the terms of their mortgage contracts.

There's nothing wrong with an adjustable-rate mortgage—if you know you're signing for it, and you plan for the adjustment when it occurs. Or if you believe you can sell the house before that adjustment occurs (in today's market? Yeah, right).

But so many people got caught unaware—which is as much their fault as the fault of the lender. Know what you're signing.

And know that you can walk away from any deal, so long as the contract is not signed *by both parties*. It's not a valid contract until both parties have affixed their legal signatures to the document.

Here are some quick and dirty things about contracts that will make your life easier in dealing with them. And before I get to them, this is the point where I must remind you that I am not an attorney and I am not giving you legal advice. I'm writing from my experience here, and I'm giving you advice, friend to friend. Realize that my advice could be wrong (hell, all of the advice in the *Guide* could be wrong. Take everything I say with a grain of salt).

So, here goes:

1. Contracts are complex legal documents.

Some are complex and incomprehensible by design. The harder it is for the layman to understand the contract, the more chances there are for that layman to get screwed. There is nothing simple about a contract. Even simple two- and three-line contracts have pitfalls in them—usually through something that's been omitted. Just because a contract looks simple doesn't mean that it is.

2. Every word in the contract is important. Each section is there for a reason.

Dean and I get into fascinating arguments about publishing contracts over this very point. Dean went to law school. He knows that some clauses in publishing contracts are completely unenforceable, so he sees no problem in signing a contract with the illegal, unenforceable clause.

I always remember the second part of two: *Each section is there for a reason.* So if the lawyers who drew up the contract knew that the clause was unenforceable (and if a guy who went to law school but never became a practicing attorney knows that a certain clause is unenforceable, then guaranteed the lawyer who put the clause in knew it as well), the question becomes: Why did the lawyers put the clause into the contract?

Usually, in publishing (and I can't say this about other industry's contracts with certainty), those clauses are there to make the ignorant do something. In the publishing contract, the ignorant one is the writer. So, the clause is often to the publishing company's benefit and it demands that the writer do something that isn't in the writer's best interest. The writer doesn't have to do that thing, because the clause is unenforceable under the contract. But I can guarantee you that if that clause is in the contract, then some writer followed "the rules" set forth by the contract, even to the writer's detriment.

So remember, everything in the contract is there for a reason—even if that reason is only to force compliance on someone who doesn't know any better.

3. Each clause in the contract has an impact on the other clauses in that contract.

An attorney friend of mine once described a contract as a story. You don't know what it all means until you get to the end.

The upside of this is that often you'll run into "dealbreakers" in the negotiation: a negotiator on the other side won't change clause A no matter what. But if you change parts of clause C & D, you'll negate A.

I learned this early on negotiating a short story contract. The contracts person told me that Clause A was unbreakable, but he said coyly, other writers have changed Clauses C & D. I read C&D and realized he was doing me a favor. He essentially gave me a way around clause A without causing him grief with his bosses and which led to me signing a much better contract.

4. Contracts bind you and the other party to a certain series of actions over time.

Contracts without a strict time limit aren't valid. In perpetuity is not a time limit. However, the time limit can be a moving target. In publishing, that moving target is often tied to the number of copies of a book sold. So if fewer than 100 copies are being sold per year, then the ticking clock of the contract sets in. In other words, the agreement between the parties may end if the book sells fewer than 100 copies for two years running. (Or some such thing.)

5. Contracts happen over a period of time.

Why did I stress that twice? Because most people look at contracts as a short-term thing, and they're usually a long-term thing.

Take our torch singer. Let's say she signed a contract with that blues club, one that guaranteed her five performance weekends per year at the club at $200 per appearance. Let's say the contract is a five-year contract.

All well and good. If she's a mediocre musician or a hobbyist, she should have no problem with that.

But what happens if her career takes off in year two? She's filling concert halls and making $20,000 appearance fees wherever she goes.

Except for that tiny blues club, which still pays her $200 per appearance, and will do so for three more years. Because she signed a bad contract. One that probably seemed good at the time.

(There are ways that a contract like that can be broken, but I'm not going to deal with them here. Generally speaking, though, if you signed a contract and so did the other party, the contract is a binding legal agreement, even if you don't like the terms two years in. In other words, you're stuck.)

6. Contracts are about control.

Control of money, control of a person's time, control of a particular property. The best contracts define the limits of that control in all areas. You may not like the definitions, but the fact that they're spelled out makes the contract understandable and negotiable. It's the simple contracts with only a few lines that get litigated most when there's a dispute over control.

7. Contracts are about the best- and worst-case scenarios.

I remember the first time I read a publishing contract. It mentions fire, flood, bankruptcy. It defines Acts of God. It discusses what to do if the publishing house goes out of business, if the writer dies, or if everyone gets sued. All the worst-case scenarios are there, including some I never thought of.

But so are the best-case scenarios: payouts if the book sells better than expected, things the publisher is obligated to do when success happens; things the writer is obligated to do.

Those lines excite writers. They think those lines mean that the publisher has changed his mind and committed to a better program for the book than initially promised. Nope. Those lines are there so that it's clear who is in control of what should the book succeed beyond anyone's wildest dreams.

8. Make sure you understand the contract you're signing.

It sounds so basic. I even mentioned that in the section above. But don't sign something you do not understand. Ask stupid questions. Repeatedly. Refuse to put your name on the document—even if there's a time crunch—until you understand every word. Better yet, don't sign unless you understand the contract's *story*, what the entire document means as a whole, not just as a sum of its parts.

Yes, I know. You didn't go to law school. Me either. But I was a reporter. And the one thing that being a reporter taught me is to question, question, question.

Contracts aren't set in stone. They can be redrafted, rewritten, redrawn. And sometimes they should be.

Whom should you ask for help with that contract? Well, that depends. Generally, you shouldn't ask the person you're negotiating with. But you shouldn't always ask your local attorney either. Because every industry has its own jargon. Publishing contracts use words that mean something different than the same words in a real estate contract.

Lawyers have specialties for a reason, and that reason is often to understand the intricacies of that specialty. I would never hire a real estate attorney to negotiate a book contract. Nor would I hire an intellectual properties attorney (who can handle a book contract) to negotiate a car loan agreement.

And even then, no matter whom I hire, I have to know that person is doing a good job. So, I need to know something of what I'm signing. The more educated I am about the contracts I sign, the better off I am.

It just so happens that I love contracts and contract negotiation. I'm fascinated by it, and I collect tons of information about publishing contracts. I knew more about publishing contracts than the agent I fired a few years ago— and he'd been in the business as long as I have.

I like publishing contracts because they're a means to an end. That end, for me, is to get my work in print. But I'm wary of contracts, too, because I've seen bad ones ruin careers.

Right now, if you're paying attention, you're watching bad contracts ruin lives. The foreclosure crisis is built on terrible deals enshrined in bad contracts.

Contracts are central to our business lives. Yet most of us know nothing about them, and certainly don't know how to negotiate them.

Now that you've read this section, you need to start familiarizing yourself with the contracts that are essential to your business. Start walking through the business sections of bookstores, look for trade journals in your field, become a devotee of places like Nolo.com. Read the free legal advice that floats around the web. Go to places where people discuss the business of doing business. Start collecting information on your specialty. It'll benefit you more than you realize.

Most of us think "I can't understand this" when it comes to contracts. Yet we have to understand it. Let me give you a tip from Colonel Tom Parker, who managed Elvis Presley— first to Elvis's benefit (in the early years) and then, when it became clear that Elvis knew nothing about money, to Parker's benefit (in the later years). Parker acknowledged that he made mistakes in negotiating contracts. He would find the clause that caused the mistake, tape it to his refrigerator, memorize it, and vow never to make that mistake again. (In later years, he put those clauses in his own contracts, and used those clauses to his own benefit.)

You will make many mistakes negotiating contracts. You won't understand all of what you sign early on. Expect to make the mistakes. Learn from them. Make sure you don't make those mistakes twice.

How To Negotiate Your Own Contract

The same day that I posted the previous section on my website, a writer asked for help with a business ethics question on one of my writer e-mail lists. Turned out her question wasn't about ethics at all. It was about a contractual relationship, a relationship defined by the contract. The answer to her question was in that contract, and negated the ethical dilemma entirely.

What was fascinating to me—and a bit appalling—was how many people answered her question as she posed it, without first wondering if she had some sort of document or contract in place. These people answered very firmly about their opinion of the ethics of the situation, when they didn't understand the situation at all.

They put me in mind of those old Holiday Inn Express commercials, in which some person steps up, gives authoritative advice that's often wrong, and then is asked if they're an expert on the situation. "Nope," they would say, "but I did stay at a Holiday Inn Express last night."

(I always wondered why the Holiday Inn Express people wanted us to stay in a place that proudly knocked off a few IQ points each time someone slept there. But hey, what do I know?)

I was rather stunned by the discussion on the list, since everyone on the list is a bright and educated person. But only one person (besides me) out of at least a dozen respondents even considered the contract, which makes me worry. These are folks who are supposed to know their freelance business, and they all made rookie mistakes that would have hurt them terribly if that "ethical" question had been theirs. The person who asked the question thought she had gone to a knowledgeable group—and it should have been—but instead she got a cross-section of America.

Most people in this country believe that business and financial matters are better dealt with by someone else, someone who is not them. Eventually, that willful ignorance catches up with everyone—and not in a pretty way.

I'll deal with the "someone elses" in the next section. In this section, I'm going to, in very vague terms, tell you the things to consider in negotiating your contract.

Before I do, I want you to do two things. If you haven't read the previous section, read it now. And I want you to remember that I am not a lawyer and I am not giving legal advice. I'm tell you how I believe the average person should think about contracts, but I'm not guaranteeing results nor am I saying that I'm always right. Essentially, I'm trying to give you a few tools so that you can go out and learn this stuff yourself.

And, if you'll note, I've often used that disclaimer or a similar one in the financial and legal sections of the *Guide*. Because I'm protecting myself here.

Some people believe that Guides like this are an implied contract. If these people follow what they believe to be my advice and the result bites them in the ass, then their first response would be to sue me. My disclaimer, here and in the other sections, is there not for those people but for any attorney that they might hire. Essentially, I'm putting the world on notice that I am not qualified to give bona fide legal advice. You're taking my advice at your own peril.

Got it?

In other words, I just did a quasi-legal document—a disclaimer—to protect me in a worst-case scenario. I've done it before, not just in the *Guide*, but also in teaching situations. If you want an expert on contracts and contract law, take classes from real attorneys. Read books written by real attorneys. Go to websites hosted by—you guessed it—real attorneys.

But I'm giving a layman's guide to negotiation, trying to give you some broad strokes and ways to think about negotiating, which is (I know) something most of you have done your very best to avoid up until now.

And that's your first mistake.

Because contracts are negotiable. In fact, most anyone who offers a contract *expects* negotiation. And not just any negotiation, but informed and intelligent negotiation.

I've known many writers who've signed horrendous contracts because the writer didn't understand that the contract should be negotiated. The writers were afraid that if they tried to negotiate, the other party would take the contract away from them, and they'd lose the deal. So, they signed.

After they signed, all of those writers had two experiences with the contract. First, the editor for the publishing house made a veiled reference to the contract, telling the writer that they "didn't get the best deal." That's editor-speak for "Oh, crap, at some point you're going to hate me, even though it'll be your fault."

Secondly, years later, those writers complained and complained and complained about being screwed. Sadly, they never realized that they had volunteered for the screwing by failing to negotiate.

So, when faced with a contract, *expect to negotiate.* That expectation will take some of the anxiety away from the whole contract experience. You know—and the person you're dealing with knows—that you both are going to discuss terms before you both sign the document.

Believe me, it's a relief to the other party when you do negotiate. Everyone wants the best possible deal in a negotiation. But if you want to work with that person or deal with that person again, you want the best possible deal that will result in other deals in the future.

When you sign a bad contract without negotiating, the other party thinks that you're naïve or really inexperienced. They hope, after you both sign, that you're just plain stupid. Because if you're stupid, you'll never wise up and you will continue to work together. If you're naïve or inexperienced, at some point you'll catch a clue, and rather than blaming yourself for failing to negotiate, you'll probably blame them for "giving" you a "bad contract."

Which means that the working relationship won't last past that moment.

People who are really worried about the future relationship will stop you just before you sign a non-negotiated contract and tell you to change a few things in the contract. Those things will be to your benefit. What's happening here is that the person you're negotiating against has just hit you with a cluestick. That person—who is your adversary in the negotiation—knows it's in his best interest to have a long-term relationship with you and is trying to protect that relationship, since you don't know enough to do it yourself.

As I write these words, I realize that a bunch of you who are reading this section have just realized that once upon a time, you were hit with that very cluestick. And most of you never caught the clue. You just thought the other person was being nice when really that person was protecting their business interests. If that person screwed you too badly—and early stage contracts are always balanced heavily toward the person issuing the contract— then that person knows you'd never work with them again.

If you've been hit with this particular cluestick and only just now realized it, get thee to books on contracts and negotiations and develop some backbone. Seriously. Because the only person you're hurting is yourself.

Not everyone you negotiate with will take care of you in a negotiation. In a one-time negotiation, where you know you don't want to or never will work with the other person again, the contract can be hideously one-sided. I watched Dean be utterly ruthless in such situations, to the point where I have to leave the room (that damn politeness again) because I really want to tell the other person that they're being screwed.

Dean is a much harder businessman than I am in these situations. He figures if the person he's negotiating against is utterly clueless, then he'll get what he wants *at their expense*. I once asked him why he's willing to do that. His answer? "They came to me."

And in each case that I observed, the other person had come to him. They initiated the relationship, they brought the product/service/idea to him and expected him to pay them for it. The fact that they did not negotiate in that situation wasn't his problem. It was theirs.

As an aside, lest you think the man is heartless, let me tell you that he never approaches someone and demands that they do business with him. And I've watched him over the years pay out much more money than he ever should to keep people in their homes, help with medical bills, and make sure they get fed.

But if someone tries to do business with him and *initiates the relationship expecting to be paid*, he will be ruthless. He expects the other person to be the same. If they're not, that's not his responsibility.

I'm not that person. But I've let him be that person as my proxy. More on this in the next section.

So, now you've decided to negotiate. But how do you do it?

Let's go back to the rules of negotiation. They are:

1. Know What You Want.
2. Ask.
3. Be Prepared to Walk Away.
4. Stay Calm.
5. Never Reveal Your Entire Hand.
6. Don't Flip-Flop.

Those tips all apply to long-term negotiation as well as short-term negotiation.

But here are some things that make negotiations over a contract different from any other kind of negotiation.

1. The contract will bind you for a certain period of time.

That period of time might be one week; it might be ten years with the possibility of renewal.

When you negotiate, that time limit needs to be first and foremost in your mind. You need to understand all the implications of it—good and bad.

Let me give you two examples. Dean, who is a great negotiator, didn't trust my experience back in 1990 or so. I knew rental agreements and the pitfalls therein. He signed an agreement for Pulphouse Publishing for a long-term lease (five years, I believe), thinking it protected him by keeping the rent at a low, low price.

I had seen too many cases where long-term rental had hurt the business in question. I got my start in real estate in 1979, when the rental market became quite competitive. Rental places offered long-term leases, but no real deals. By 1981, as the recession deepened, many places forfeited their leases, and the rental companies lowered their rates for commercial properties. Sometimes they gave months away for free just for signing up. The companies that signed the agreement in 1979 paid five times what a company did in 1981.

That was part of my argument to Dean. He said he could live with that risk. But the other part of my argument was we might go out of business, and if we did, we would still be on the hook for that five-year lease. At the time, our business was going gangbusters. He did not believe that we would be gone within two years.

We were. And we were stuck with that lease. Fortunately for us, the landlord never fixed up the property and a friend got injured because of his negligence. That allowed Dean to negotiate a settlement, negating the rental agreement. But he wouldn't have had to do that if he had negotiated the term of the agreement down to a year or so, renewable on the same terms.

Who was right in this instance? Neither of us, really. Because had the business remained successful, then Dean's gamble would have paid off. Commercial real estate rental rates in Eugene, Oregon, climbed in that five-year period, and if we had to renew every year, we ran the risk of having our rent hiked dramatically.

The time limit on a contract can benefit you and it can hurt you. What looks like a good deal now might be a bad deal in the future.

It's up to you to imagine all the scenarios outlined in that contract, and decide if you can live with them ten, twenty, fifty years from now.

I deal with this a lot with writer friends. At various points in the career, writers can be short of money. Early on, writers are often broke, and that's when they sign bad contacts—particularly with Hollywood.

"Small Hollywood money," as one of my ex-agents called it, can run anywhere from $10,000 to $150,000. Those figures sound like a lot to most people, but to the suits in Hollywood, that's pocket change. I've had friends get "mediocre" Hollywood deals that ran from $200,000 to $700,000. And of course, the "good" deals go higher than that.

The key to Hollywood deals isn't the money. It's the terms of the contract. Often those $50,000 contracts have some nasty, nasty clauses. Clauses that say no matter what, the 50K is all the writer will ever get. (There are other nasty clauses not relevant here, but man, could I tell you stories…)

I've known a lot of writers who are really, really broke who need that $50,000 desperately. And before they sign that contract, I ask them this question, "Will you be happy twenty years from now after that project you got paid 50K for has become a blockbuster movie? Everyone else on the project will have made millions and will continue to make millions. You will have 50K that probably disappeared within the first two years you had it. If you can live with that scenario, then sign the contract."

Because, folks, the worst-case scenario in a contract like that is *success*. Most people step back, think about it, and decide to negotiate—trying to get some fees from later parts of that pie. But I have known a handful who either gambled that the 50K was all the project would ever make or who needed the money so badly that they knew, even twenty years hence, that they could live with the decision.

All of those factors influence negotiation.

You need a lot of imagination when faced with a contract. You have to imagine the worst-case and best-case scenarios for you. And you need to know how you'll feel about them for the duration of that contract.

In other words, you need to know yourself very, very well.

In most instances, I could walk away from that 50K no matter how desperate I was, because I know I'd be angry about it (with myself) twenty years from now. But in a circumstance that's life or death—paying for a surgery, for example—I'd accept that 50K in a heartbeat, and deal with the consequences later.

It's all very fluid.

What you need to figure is where you're at now, where you hope to be in the future, and what impact the decisions you make today will have on that future.

Because once you sign the contract, it's binding. And if you think negotiation is hard at this stage, imagine doing it—as Dean did—after the contract was signed and agreed to, and your circumstances changed for the worse. Then the negotiation is really, really, really hard—and might even take you to court. If you do go to court, and you have a valid contract signed by both parties, then you'll lose the case, guaranteed.

Negotiate up front when it's expected and it's relatively easy.

2. Focus on what you want.

When you enter into a contractual negotiation, know what you want and protect it. Don't get sidelined by other things.

For example, I want control over my work. I will walk away from contracts that take the control away from me—unless I'm asked to work in someone else's universe, like Star Trek or Star Wars. In those cases, I know that I'm entering a world that someone else controls, and I'll forfeit rights that I'll fight to the death for over my original work.

I've walked away from very lucrative contracts because I would lose control over my original work. I've accepted financially small contracts that have given me a lot of creative control. Control of my own work matters the most to me.

Other writers want publication more than anything. I watched a writer sign one of the worst contracts I'd ever seen because he was desperate to be published. When told how bad the contract was, he claimed he knew, but didn't care. Publication was the only thing that mattered to him.

Know what you want out of that agreement. Know how far you will go to protect what you want as you negotiate that agreement. Make sure you protect what you want *throughout the term* (time limit) of the agreement.

Everything else in the agreement is gravy, then.

3. Make sure you have a way to terminate the contract.

Often the termination clause benefits whoever drew up the contract. I've seen rental agreements in which the landlord can terminate the agreement with 24 hours notice, while the renter had to give six months notice. (Those agreements were so egregious that the State of Wisconsin stepped in and mandated a 30-day termination in all rental agreements, but each state is different.)

I've seen publishing contracts where the publisher can easily cancel the contract but the writer has to jump through so many hoops to cancel it that it would take months to even try.

Make sure the termination clause is clear and equitable. By equitable I mean that it's either very hard for both sides to terminate or very easy for both sides to terminate. But it shouldn't be easy for one side and hard for the other.

4. Money.

Most people mistakenly think that contracts are all about money. But remember what I said in the previous section. Contracts are about *control*.

So…

5. Make sure you know how you'll get paid or how you will make the payments.

That sounds so elementary, but it's not. Many contracts may promise a lot of money, but if you read the fine print, you'll realize that certain payments will get made if and only if other conditions are met. Some of those conditions might be extremely unlikely to ever occur.

For example, Hollywood contracts often promise to pay a percentage of "net profits." But anyone peripherally attached to Hollywood knows that "net profits" never happen. Creative bookkeeping will make certain that even the highest earning films make no net profit, although they'll have a gross profit. (And if you don't understand the difference between those terms, get *How To Make Money: A Freelancer's Guide Short Book*)

So, the contract promising to pay x% of net profit really promises nothing.

Publishing has its own accounting tricks, which I could spend the next several weeks enumerating for you, everything from basket accounting to high discount rates.

Yet there are reasons to sign such contracts, and often those reasons have more to do with what you want than what you'll get paid. You might get other clauses in the contract that will make you feel better about dodgy payment practices.

6. Control As Much of the Contract As Possible.

Remember that's what you and the other party are negotiating—who controls what. Try to keep as much of that control in your court as you possibly can. But realize where you stand and who you're negotiating with. For example, if you're negotiating a contract to sell your work to the movies, realize that you don't have the deep pockets to make the film yourself. You will have to relinquish some control in those areas so that the film will get made. Just like they'll have to reimburse you for your property if they really, really want it. (And want to control it.)

7. Once you both sign, negotiation is over.

It's your signature on that document. That means you agreed to the terms therein. You *agreed*. The time to change the terms is before you sign. If you complain afterwards, you won't get any sympathy from me or anyone else who understands contracts. Because understanding that document is your responsibility and you must understand it before you sign it.

Even more important, you must know you can live with the contract's terms for the duration of that contract, be it six months or sixty years.

If you sign it, you're responsible for every word in it. You've made your bed, as my mother used to say—and the contract is proof of that.

I could go on and on and on forever. Contracts are exceedingly complicated. Law schools spend several semesters on contracts. But, in short, here are some of the basics of contract negotiation (covered above):

1. Expect to Negotiate A Contract.

2. Imagine How the Terms of the Contract Will Impact You Over the Lifetime of the Contract.

3. Focus on What You Want.

4. Make Sure You Have An Equitable Way to Terminate The Contract.

5. Make Sure You Know How You'll Get Paid or How You Will Make Payments.

6. Control As Much of the Contract As Possible.

7. Once You Both Sign, Negotiation Is Over.

Good contracts, bad contracts, beautifully negotiated contracts, non-negotiated contracts—ultimately what happens with those is all up to you.

Expect no help with contracts. Learn it all yourself. I'll deal with this aspect more in the next section, but remember this: *You are responsible for your own career*—the good and the bad. Just you. And that responsibility extends to the agreement you make and the contracts you sign.

When to Hire Someone Else to Negotiate Your Contract

or
Agents, Lawyers, and Business Managers (Oh, My)

In the previous sections, I've talked about the things you need to know about yourself and your business in order to negotiate anything from a weekend gig to a long-term contract. I've mentioned managers, agents, and lawyers in passing—people whom you can hire to negotiate for you—but I've pretty much skipped over what they do in favor of having you do it yourself.

In fact, if you read the entire *Freelancer's Survival Guide*, you'll see me recommend time and time again that you should do most of this stuff, from the financial to negotiation, yourself.

Yet, I have a book agent and quite often I bring him into a book deal for the express purpose of negotiation. He negotiates the deal for me.

Does that make me a hypocrite? Am I telling you to do what I say, not what I do?

No. Just this week—which is, for those of you reading this late, the week between Christmas and New Years 2009-2010, I negotiated a contract all by my lonesome. It was a short e-rights contract for a novella that a publisher wanted to include in an anthology. The contract was purposely short and very vague (see the section about Understanding Contracts to understand why someone would want to do that), and I made it less vague. But I still left in points a hard negotiator would have changed.

Why? Because, in this case—and this case only—it was in my best interest to keep that contract simple. Normally, I would have negotiated that little contract bloody. But I saw a greater benefit in keeping the contract loose on both sides than I did in pinning everything down.

Also this week, I've read a contract of Dean's, giving him some feedback (which he really didn't need because he's so good at this stuff) and helped him design an agreement for another project he's working on.

And that doesn't count the several approaches I had from people who want something—a free story (no), a guest appearance (maybe), or some other thing that will require negotiation.

Normally, I handle so many negotiations that I barely pay attention to how many. I'm used to it now. These past ten days have been relatively slow in the negotiation department.

Finally, this week, I'm reading—slowly—a book contract for one of my pen names. The contract is with a brand-new company for me and is the fourth iteration of the agreement. We've been negotiating since the first of November, or I should say, my agent has been doing so, while keeping me informed.

The day before Christmas, he e-mailed me the latest iteration, with all of his e-mails and the company's responses, so that I could see what had been done so far. I'm reading this version over the holidays, with the idea that there will be one, maybe two, maybe three more iterations before we're done.

My agent is a good negotiator, a man with a law degree who has a fondness for contract law and for publishing contracts, in particular. He's good and sharp and catches things I might miss (or might not care as much about as I should). But in all of the contracts that he's negotiated for me so far, I've added language, cut language, or asked for things he never even considered. I'm very, very hands-on, even though he's the one interacting with the company.

I'm walking all sorts of negotiating lines in what is a relatively slow week, from negotiating contracts myself to making agreements by e-mail to making some verbal agreements to hiring someone to do the negotiations for me. That's normal in a small business. Negotiation is, as I've said before, part of everyday life. You need to get used to it.

The trick is to know when to do the negotiation yourself and when to hire someone. Once you hire someone to negotiate for you, you must manage that negotiator properly.

First, let's discuss knowing when to hire someone. I discussed this briefly when talking about a torch singer who was asked to play a local club. I showed the torch singer's various considerations as she negotiated her fee and her performance time at that club.

As to whether she should hire someone to negotiate for her, I said this:

At her level of the career, it would be foolish for her to hire a manager to do the negotiating for her. Better that she learn how to do it on her own than sacrifice $15 to $20 of that much needed $100 for someone to speak for her—when she wouldn't get much out of that deal anyway.

Many of the considerations for hiring a negotiator are present in that short paragraph. Let's look at them.

1) What can a negotiator bring to the table?

That's always the first question you should ask. Sometimes all the negotiator brings is *a calm, disinterested voice*. And in some cases, that calm, disinterested voice is worth every penny you spend on it. A person who is not emotionally involved should—and let me emphasize *should*—see things a bit more clearly and hear what the other party has to say without bias.

This calm disinterest is often why many organizations hire arbitrators to help negotiate contracts between say, a union and a company. The arbitrator will not negotiate for either side, but will facilitate negotiations. In these instances, each side has its own negotiator and the negotiator works through an arbitrator, to keep things as calm and above-board as possible.

Generally speaking, you as a freelancer don't need that high level of expertise. But you do need to figure out what you need. If a calm voice is all that's necessary, then you might not need a professional negotiator at all.

Let me stop one more time here and say this, *a professional negotiator has a different name in different businesses*. Lawyers can be professional negotiators. Most people in publishing rely on agents. People in Hollywood have tiers of negotiators from agents to managers to lawyers. Singers often have managers. But even your accountant can and will negotiate for you with the IRS, if need be. So, negotiators come with all sorts of professional labels. For the purpose of this section, I will call them negotiators.

What else can the negotiator bring to the table? *Expertise.* It might take the negotiator five minutes to negotiate a contract that you'll struggle over for days, simply because the negotiator is more familiar with the language of that contract than you are.

A negotiator can also bring *clout.* Some negotiators— agents and managers in particular—have a reputation all their own, over and above yours. That reputation should augment the negotiation in a good way. In other words, if you're a beginner like that torch singer, a high-powered manager might—might—get you more money just because he's on board. He might be able to get you into meetings with prospective clients that you wouldn't otherwise get.

A negotiator also has the ability *to say things you can't.* That might sound silly until you think about it. I would love to tell a publisher that he should pay me more because I'm pretty or famous or a damned fine writer, but it sounds better when my representative says it. Right now, as a woman who has worked in this field for twenty years and has many accolades as well as an excellent track record, I'm a lot more comfortable doing this part for myself. But even now, I don't say, "I'm a bestselling, award-winning writer. You should pay me more." I'm a lot more subtle than that. But I do make sure that the party I'm negotiating with has the facts before she begins bargaining with me, so that when I get to my way of dealing with this, which is, "It's not standard practice for me to accept a fee that low or this particular term in a contract," she knows I'm coming from a position of strength.

Early on, you might have to hire that strength. Or someone willing to make that statement for you.

There is a downside to everything a negotiator can bring to the table. Right now, I'm only discussing the upside. But you'll have to factor it all in, including the screw-up factor, which is this:

The more people you bring into a negotiation, the more likely it is to go wrong.

A long chain of negotiators (often seen in Hollywood—the lawyer talks to the manager who talks to the agent [or doesn't, as the case may be]) can turn a negotiation into one ugly game of telephone.

And in the end, the only person who'll suffer for it is you.

But I get ahead of myself.

In answering the *what does the negotiator bring to the table* question, you have to be realistic. Often, a negotiator adds nothing to a negotiation. If you're savvy about your own business, you probably have all the skills you need to negotiate, and bringing someone else in just muddies the waters. In the case of our torch singer, a negotiator wouldn't bring anything to the table except calm, which wasn't worth the fee the torch singer would have to pay for that calm.

So, before hiring a negotiator for a particular job, make sure the negotiator adds value. So many people have someone negotiate just because that person is on the payroll or that's what they have this particular worker for, without thinking about whether or not the negotiator is even appropriate to the circumstance.

Think before you act. And think twice before you hire someone. Or maybe three or four times.

2. In this instance, make sure the negotiator is worth his fee.

Again, you're looking at value, but you're looking at it from a slightly different perspective. If you look at the case of our torch singer, you'll remember she really needed the money from that gig to pay her rent. Taking ten to twenty-five percent of the fee away to pay a manager at that point would have been financially devastating for her.

It's better for her to do the negotiation herself and keep the money than it is to bring in a third party.

This is a two-pronged decision, by the way. I have a rule of thumb for my business. Under a certain dollar amount, I generally handle the negotiations myself. Over that amount, I *consider* bringing in my agent. I don't always do so.

But it's only a rule of thumb. If there's something I really, really, really want in that negotiation, something that's so important that I'll walk if I don't get it, I'm more likely to bring in the third party to negotiate for me. Partly, this is so that I won't tip my hand. Partly, it's to keep emotions out of the way, and partly, it's because I'm a pessimist. In that particular instance, I expect to walk away. I don't want to be the one to tell the company that we can't come to an agreement. I want my representative to do that—because that falls into the category of something I would rather have someone else say for me than saying it myself.

When you're considering the fee, you have to look at the value the negotiator will bring. I once had a writer friend tell me he was "training" his accountant to work with someone in the arts. In other words, my friend was paying someone who brought no value to the table and who, in fact, was costing my friend not just money but time as well. The accountant had no expertise in the area that my friend needed and therefore was making a boatload of money that my friend could have easily kept for himself.

In the case of our torch singer, the manager wouldn't have gotten her any more money. He probably wouldn't have gotten a better deal. He would simply have finalized the negotiation and taken anywhere from ten to twenty-five percent to do so. If she hired a manager in that instance, she was throwing her money away.

Let's look briefly at the flipside: my book contract. My agent has put in a lot of work negotiating boilerplate and other points to the contract. A great deal of my time over the past two months would have gone to minutia that I would have negotiated as well, but I didn't have to. It's been worth the fee.

However, I am reviewing that work right now and will add my own opinions shortly. But in value, which I'm equating with service in exchange for money, I'm getting my money's worth.

The tricky thing is that each negotiation is different. Even my rule of thumb doesn't always work—which is why I look at it as a rule of thumb instead of something hard and fast.

In short, I bring in a negotiator *only when I need one*. I don't use a negotiator just because I happen to have one at the ready. I use one only when necessary.

Here's the other side of negotiating: so much can go wrong. You will make mistakes, as I've said before. But it's better for *you* to make the mistake than your negotiator.

Because if you're truly hands-off in negotiation, you might not know about the mistake until the negotiation is over and you've signed the contract. And that, my friends, is not your negotiator's fault. It's your fault.

Let me quote a comment left when I made the first negotiation post on my website. It's from Randy Tatano, who works as a freelance broadcast news reporter, mostly for NBC.

He wrote:

Well, on the topic of hiring someone to negotiate, a news anchor I know hired an agent to negotiate her next contract. Her agent took such a hard line that management called her bluff and she ended up out of work. She had absolutely no desire to leave but apparently didn't convey that well enough to her agent.

On the other side I was trying to hire an anchor once and the agent was so incredibly obnoxious I moved on to someone else. I was trying to negotiate and meet the guy in the middle but he wanted to play hardball.

What surprised me about these instances is that both anchors were extremely likable people, yet hired agents who were so difficult to deal with. And, as you pointed out so well Kris, anyone who negotiates for you needs to know exactly how you feel.

He's right. Too often a negotiator, who thinks he's acting in your best interest, can really cause damage to you and your business. Whose fault is that? Not the negotiator's. It's yours. You might have hired the wrong person, brought the negotiator into a situation he had no business being a part of, or failed to communicate what you really wanted from that negotiator.

As I was getting ready to write this section, I found all kinds of horrible stuff about the people you can hire to do tasks for you. The universe seemed to serve up these stories. Some will factor in later in this section.

But let me share one right now. In the *Washington Post* on January 5, 2010, toward the end of an article about the IRS regulating tax preparers ("IRS to Regulate Paid Preparers of Tax Returns to Reduce Errors," by David S. Hilzenrath), I found these interesting statistics: In 2006, employees of the Government Accountability Office, posing as taxpayers, had tax prep chains fill out tax returns. "All 19 preparers made mistakes, the IRS reported. Only two of the 19 arrived at the correct bottom line."

Ten of the 19 didn't report income they'd been told about and "several" didn't ask about income other than wages—in other words, stuff you as a freelancer would earn.

A 2008 study got similar if slightly better results. Seventeen out of 28 preparers got the bottom line wrong, leaving eleven instead of two to get the results right.

The IRS estimates that somewhere around 1 million people prepare taxes for a fee, and many do that without being tested. As IRS Commissioner Douglas Shulman said, "In most states you need a license to cut someone's hair, [but today] most tax-return preparers don't have to meet *any standards* when they sit down and prepare a federal tax return…." (Emphasis mine.)

What is it with this country and its regulations? My ex-husband got a job as a financial adviser without finishing college by taking a two-week course, and with our own finances in such a mess that *I* wasn't taking advice from him. Book agents across the country have absolutely no regulation, and yet writer after writer puts their entire livelihood in an agent's hands, often without oversight.

Now this about tax preparers. Since I only had someone prepare my taxes once—and that was because I was broke and in those days tax preparers were the only ones who could e-file and I needed the damn refund yesterday—I never investigated this in-depth. (And essentially Dean and I handed the tax preparer the finished tax return. She just e-filed it for us.)

Apparently, in the United States of America, you have to follow rules for everything *unless* you want to handle other people's money. Oh, I can't tell you how deeply that appalls me.

Yet time and time again, people tell me how happy they are to hire someone so that they don't have to think about business. And I think when they say that, *You need to get out of business now and go work a day job. Because you're setting yourself up to get screwed.*

So…after reading the *Guide*, you're smart enough to track your own finances and to bring in a negotiator only when you need one.

But are you smart enough to supervise that negotiator properly?

What? What's this "supervise" word? Isn't the negotiator the expert?

Well, no. It's your business. Therefore, you're the expert. The negotiator is just your mouthpiece.

Let's go back to Randy Tatano's comment from above. Look at this part of that comment:

…a news anchor I know hired an agent to negotiate her next contract. Her agent took such a hard line that

*management called her bluff and she ended up out of work.
She had absolutely no desire to leave but apparently didn't
convey that well enough to her agent.*

There's a lot in that tiny paragraph. I'm not going to make
any assumptions about the anchor here because I don't know
her. But here's what I get:

The anchor wanted something in her next contract.
Maybe she wanted more money, maybe she wanted a better
on-air time. Maybe she wanted a half-hour monthly program
showcasing her talent. Who knows?

But whatever it was, she told the agent—the negotiator—
about it. What she did *not* say was that this particular thing
that she wanted—for the sake of argument, let's say it's
more money—was flexible. In other words, it was not a deal
breaker.

Clearly, though, the agent did not know that. He thought
the goal of the negotiation was to get that extra money—not to
keep the anchor's job. So, when management didn't cough up
the extra cash (or whatever it was), the agent walked. (See the
section on negotiation options.)

Only the client didn't want to walk. She wanted to keep
the job.

What we have here, folks, is a failure to communicate.

And another problem.

The agent acted without consulting the client. He walked
without telling her, and she lost that job.

Did the agent do a bad job? You could say so, since the
anchor didn't get whatever it was that she wanted. But I'll

wager that the agent did a fine job. The problem here, as I see it, is with the client.

Because she did not communicate her needs up front to the person negotiating for her.

I've had agents go off half-cocked on me, especially when I was younger. (And I even had an agent who called me "hon," which should've been a red flag that he didn't respect me, but I was too young to realize it. Besides, back then, every man who was more than ten years older than me called me "hon" or "dear." I had no idea that an employee shouldn't do that.) I had one who set my bottom line at $15,000 per project. That agent rejected projects without telling me. And when I found that out, that agent no longer worked for me.

Now, my poor current agent suffers from my past mistakes and those of the people I hired. I must seem a bit paranoid to him. I keep track of everything from rejections to offers. And I keep the most track during negotiations.

How do I do that?

Simple. I have a hard and fast set of rules. And they aren't for the negotiator. They're for me.

Before anyone enters into a negotiation for me, I go through these steps:

1. I figure out what I want out of the negotiation.

If I were that news anchor, I'd figure out which I wanted more—the money (or whatever it was) or the job. In her case, it was clearly the job. So, that's the primary goal of the negotiation. I would tell the agent to make sure I keep that job, no matter what.

2. I figure out how far I'm willing to bend.

No matter how much I want the job, am I willing to sell myself short to get it (or keep it)? Do I have other prospects that are as good or better? Do I really want to work with these people? How much leeway do I have in this negotiation? Can I walk?

3. Are there any deal-breakers?

For me, there are always deal-breakers. There are clauses in publishing contracts that I will not sign, even if I'm on my last dime and starving to death. As I mentioned in earlier sections, most of those clauses have to do with control, not with money. If my name (or one of my names) appears on the work, then I'd better approve of that work. And that's my bottom line.

4. What kind of tone do I want to set?

Randy alludes to this in another part of his comments. He says, *On the other side I was trying to hire an anchor once and the agent was so incredibly obnoxious I moved on to someone else.* I prefer a civil tone in my negotiations, but I've been known to hire sharks on occasion—folks who are just vicious in negotiation. (I even got rid of one shark for not having enough bite.) Sometimes that hard line is very important to me. Sometimes the tone has to be very, very soft. Again, it varies according to circumstance, which is often why I handle some negotiations on my own. The *tone* is too difficult to explain easily, so I just do it myself.

Once I've figured out what I want, I must communicate all of that to my negotiator. I used to do that on the phone or in person, but soon learned that in business as in life, people hear what they want to hear. So now, I write this all into a letter or into an e-mail, so that the negotiator can refer to it during the negotiations.

Then, before anything goes any farther, I make sure that my negotiator understands my needs and *agrees with them.* This sounds so silly, since the negotiator is essentially an employee, but often the negotiator, hired for his skill, forgets that.

The agent I had who set the $15,000 limit forgot who was in charge. That agent believed I needed to write slower, and in order to "force" me to write slower (since I clearly wasn't doing it on my own), the agent set that arbitrary 15K limit on my work, thinking if I got paid that as a minimum, I'd slow down. Now, honestly, how many of you can live on 15K per year? I certainly can't. In all fairness, I had told the agent *on one project* that I would take no less than 15K, and that agent heard me set that as a limit for all of my projects. But I know that agent had been trying to get me to slow down for some time, and this was a case of hearing what you wanted to hear.

See why I write things down?

I've had negotiators tell me that they'll never take on a negotiation that they can't walk away from. Which tells me these are people I don't want to hire. Because I don't always want to walk from a negotiation, just like that anchor didn't above. Which means that this type of negotiator is wrong for me.

Once I'm convinced the negotiator and I are on the same page, then I let the negotiator do his job. But I keep a watchful eye on the proceedings. And here's the real key:

The negotiator must check with me before making any decision.

I *never* give the negotiator the ability to make choices for me. That means that the negotiator *must* present me with any offer that crosses his desk, even if he does not approve of that offer.

I've had negotiators tell me that "we got this offer, and I don't think we should take it." In that case, I have the negotiator tell me what the offer is and why he thinks I shouldn't agree to it. I always listen, but I don't always act on the advice.

Because it is my business and I know what I want from that business, much better than the negotiator ever will.

Sometimes, of course, I should have listened. But more often than not, I ended up making the right choice—because I had possession of all the facts.

I keep track of the negotiation.

I stay in the loop. Even thought I've given my negotiator the outlines of what I want, I know that negotiation is not a linear process. First, I need to know that the general terms are agreed to by both sides. But a negotiation can go awry on the smallest of details, some that don't appear until late in the contract phase.

So, I keep track.

When my negotiator thinks we have a deal, I get all aspects of that deal from him, and then I examine that deal with a fine-tooth comb. As I mentioned above, I often find things that were missed.

In some cases, I find things I just don't understand. I research them. First, I ask my negotiator what he believes they mean. Then, I look into it myself.

One agent that I hired hated this about me. We received a contract for a book deal that I really didn't like, but he felt we should accept it because the publisher had gone to the trouble of issuing the contract. That contract had a few dealbreakers in it for me, things I had mentioned to the agent up front, things he couldn't get the publisher to budge on. The contract came, I asked again, the publisher wouldn't budge, and I refused to sign. The deal was off.

The agent got angry with me, and that was the end of our relationship. He did not have the ability to walk away at all stages of the deal, and that harmed my business.

But I remembered the primary rule of negotiation:

It's my signature that goes on the contract; I'm the one who must live with the deal—not the negotiator. So therefore, if I don't like it and I can't fix it, I don't agree to it.

Period.

End of story.

So, I get a preliminary final contract and I go through it carefully. Often I'll negotiate other points—through my negotiator, of course. And I outline those points as carefully as I outlined the early stage of the negotiation.

I tell the negotiator if there are any dealbreakers in the final points. I tell the negotiator if I'd sign the contract *as is*, but that I'd like these points if we can get them. I'm very clear about where I stand at that point in the negotiation, so that the negotiator is clear, too.

Finally, because it bears repeating, *I never agree to a deal that I do not understand.* I can't tell you how many times I've had a negotiator tell me to trust them, they did the best they could, and the deal can't get any better. (That early agent actually said, "Trust me, honey.") All of that might be true—the negotiator may have done the best they could. The deal might not get better. But often the things I ask for in the latter stages of the negotiation *never even came up* in the early stages. The negotiator might not have gotten a better deal *because the negotiator didn't know he should try.*

If you keep track of the negotiator and the negotiation, you will be able to tell how good a job your negotiator is doing for you. You'll know, for example, if the other party is getting angry at your negotiator (as in Randy's example, above.) In that case, you might be able to step in and salvage the negotiation. I've done that once or twice.

You'll also find out if your negotiator is as big an expert as she claims to be. A friend of mine hired a book agent who had worked as a book editor first. That agent claimed to know contracts.

By the time my friend got the final contract, that agent had added a mountain of clauses. (Added clauses are in bold.) *All of those clauses benefited the publisher, not the writer. All* of them. That agent knew contracts, all right. She knew them from the publishing side of the equation, not the writing side, but she didn't understand the legal language at all. If she had, she would have known that she was hurting her client, not helping him.

Unfortunately for my friend, he had a trust-me agent. (I wonder if she actually patted him on the head and said, "Trust me, honey.") And he trusted her instead of his writer friends who told him not to sign that contract, and who told him to negotiate a better one. As a result, this friend has signed the worst contract I have ever seen for a novel in my thirty years of publishing. And the sad part is that the worst clauses were added *by his negotiator.*

See why I tell you that you must know more about your business than anyone else? Why I tell you to understand what you sign? Yes, that means you must know a bit about the law as it pertains to your business, about the contracts that you will inevitably sign. As you can see from the examples from the newspaper, you must also understand the tax implications of your business, and how to handle your own money.

And you must supervise your employees—including the "experts" that you hire. The most important one to supervise (after your accountant and people who actually touch your money) is your negotiator, be she a lawyer, a manager, an agent, or your second-in-command.

You can't become a freelancer to avoid the business world. When you're a freelancer, you need to know more about business than everyone around you.

You must remember that your negotiator represents *you.* Your negotiator speaks for you. If you want her to speak in harsh tones, then hire a shark. If you want her to speak in soft tones, hire a more personable negotiator. Do not hire a pushover. Ever. Which means that you will occasionally have run-ins with your negotiator. If there is a run-in, make sure you win. If the negotiator balks, then you fire that negotiator and hire a different one.

Negotiators work *for you* and *must* have your best interest in mind.

Note I didn't state the cliché and say that they should have your best interest at heart. They have their own best interest at heart. Ultimately, a negotiator is in business for herself. But if she wants to do a good job for you, then she must do the job you hired her for *and nothing else*. And she must know where she stands.

So, let me reiterate.

If you decided to hire a negotiator, then here's how you supervise that person:

1. Communicate what you want out of the negotiation in writing.
2. Make sure your negotiator understands what you want before proceeding with the negotiation.
3. The negotiator cannot make decisions on her own. She must check with you before agreeing to anything.
4. Supervise the negotiation. Be hands on.

5. Make sure you understand all the details of the negotiated deal before agreeing to anything.

6. Remember that you are bound by the deal, not your negotiator. No matter what your negotiator recommends, you do not sign (or agree to) the final deal unless you understand it and can live with its terms.

You can fire a negotiator in the middle of a negotiation. (Be aware that it might have an impact on your bargaining power, however.) You can step into that negotiation at any point and do all the work yourself. You do not need someone to negotiate for you. And if you do hire someone to negotiate for you, make sure they negotiate *for you*, and not for themselves or someone else.

This short book on negotiation has given you a lot to think about and a lot to remember, I know. Negotiation is both an art and a science, and it's critical to all forms of business. Learn your own strengths and weaknesses in negotiation. Once you know what they are, you'll know when to hire help and when to forego it.

But even if you do hire someone to speak for you, stay informed and make sure they're speaking your words, not theirs. Because a negotiator can screw up a deal badly without even realizing it, as in Randy Tatano's example. A negotiator can also bind you to a deal you don't want, as in my friend's trust-me agent case.

In both cases, those negotiators were poorly supervised. In the case of the anchor, it's up for debate whether she should have hired that particular negotiator. In the case of my writer friend, he hired a bad negotiator who made the situation much, much worse. He would have been better off signing the publisher's boilerplate contract without any negotiation at all.

So, hire someone to speak for you with trepidation, knowing that the negotiator can muck things up. Make sure you're hiring that person for the right reasons. And keep a close eye on the proceedings.

You'll be happy you did.

About the Author

Award-winning, bestselling writer Kristine Kathryn Rusch has published books under many names and in many genres. She has owned several businesses, and has worked for herself for more than thirty years. For more information on her work, go to http://www.kristinekathrynrusch.com.

If you found this section of Kristine Kathryn Rusch's The Freelancer's Survival Guide *helpful, you might want these short books as well:*

Getting Started
Goals and Dreams
How To Make Money
Networking in Person And Online
Time Management
The Secrets of Success
Turning Setbacks into Opportunity
When to Quit Your Day Job

List of all the
Freelancer's Survival Guide
Short Books

When to Quit Your Day Job
Getting Started
Turning Setbacks into Opportunity
Goals and Dreams
How to Negotiate Anything
The Secrets of Success
How to Make Money
Networking in Person and Online
Time Management

These books can be found in many bookstores in both electronic and paper editions. For more information, please go to www.WMG Publishing.com

WMG
Publishing

CPSIA information can be obtained
at www.ICGtesting.com
Printed in the USA
LVOW12s1553100418
572940LV00001B/66/P